Online Marketing Animal Hospitals, Simplified

Everything you need to know to get started

Andrew P. Laine

Contents

Thinking about hiring an agency?

Earlier this year, I attended an industry conference where I had the opportunity to chat with a group of practice owners about their marketing strategies over dinner. To say the least, it was an eye opening experience that eventually served as my motivation to write this book. What I saw that night was a group of practitioners who were passionate about their practices, but frustrated and confused about if and how they should attack the Internet. They knew all of the right buzzwords, like "Facebook," "Twitter," "SEO," and "Blogging," but they couldn't verbalize any semblance of a strategy for using these online tools to grow their practices. I was baffled to find that a few were even paying upwards of $10,000 a year to advertise in the Yellow Pages!

These days, many veterinarians who feel out of place in marketing are turning to marketing agencies to help them develop and carry out an online marketing strategy. But, I have to ask, when is the last time you heard another practice owner or manager telling a success story about what one of these companies did for them? The truth is, while marketing agencies and contractors do offer important services, there are two primary reasons that you should think twice before working with one:

1) Marketing agencies typically take a standardized approach to marketing your practice. In other words, they're not likely to put much time or effort into building customized campaigns for you. You need to understand that what's most important to them is to lock you into a long-term service agreement upfront, and then finish whatever they promised to do for you in as little time as possible each month.

2) While they'll attract your interest with the idea of growing your practice, rarely will they agree to a payment plan based on the sales they generate for your business. That's not because they're dishonest—it's because they don't know whether their approach will actually produce results, and they don't want to

work for free. Doing it yourself, on the other hand, gives you the flexibility to find what works through trial and error for free, and then focus on it relentlessly.

That said, if you really don't want to do it yourself, and you can afford an agency's fees, working with one might be a good option. If that's not the case for you, however, I have good news! By spending a little time each week focusing on your practice's online marketing plan, you can *do it yourself* and save thousands of dollars on what you'd spend paying someone else to do it. Don't get me wrong, every successful marketing campaign requires some sort of investment—time, energy, money, etc.—but if you're willing to try, most of the time you're going to see a sizeable return.

In fact, it is my sincere hope that after reading this short e-book that you'll have a basic understanding of internet marketing that you can use to start creating an actionable online marketing strategy today. So, from here on out, I'll walk you through the world of online marketing step-by-step, eventually helping you to: 1) set up a website that reflects well on your practice while satisfying your visitors' needs; 2)

understand how search engines work so you can start putting together a

Search Engine Optimization (SEO) strategy and begin buying targeted

search ads; and 3) start using social networks like Facebook, Twitter,

and YouTube to interact with and grow your client base—essentially

everything you need to know to succeed at online marketing.

An Introduction to Online Marketing

The majority of your clients own a smartphone, tablet, laptop or desktop computer, and use it regularly to find information about how to care for their pets. Did you know, for example, that in the United States there are over 2.7 million unique Google searches each month for the keyword "Animal Hospital"? Even localized searches like "Phoenix Animal Hospital" are conducted thousands of times per month. More than 1.5 million pet owners have opted to receive regular updates from Petsmart.com on Facebook, and millions more look to YouTube for how-to videos and tutorials that will teach them how to take care of their pets.

The point is that we live in an age where people know that they can turn to the Internet when they have questions. Whether they're looking for reviews of local pet hospitals, or trying to find out what it will cost them to have the dog's teeth cleaned, they know that someone else in the world has probably asked the same question and posted the answer online. The potential for practicing veterinarians to reach potential clients online is simply astounding!

Online marketing is an opportunity to position your practice in a way that allows you to help people find the answers to their questions and live better lives. When you do, they'll trust you more, and be more likely to turn to you when their pets need care. You must only keep in mind that "positioning yourself" online is not as passive as it sounds; it's an active, ongoing process that means engaging with people and making it increasingly easier for them to find information about your company. Putting up a website, signing up for Facebook and Twitter accounts, and sending out occasional practice newsletters are necessary steps, but they're not enough. Rather, online marketing is about finding ways to connect over and over again and to continue to provide valuable resources to people who are looking for them. That's what this e-book is going to help you do.

A preliminary assessment

Before we get into the nuts and bolts of a DIY online marketing plan, let's start with a simple 10-question assessment of your current online strategy. Hopefully it will give you an idea of where you stand, and where you have room to improve.

1) Does your practice's website have a blog?

   - Yes (10 points)

   - No (5 points)

   - My practice doesn't even have a website. (0 points)

2) How often do you post content to your blog?

   - At least once per week (10 points)

   - 1-3 times per month (5 points)

   - Rarely, if ever (0 points)

3) Does your practice have a Facebook fanpage?

   - Yes (10 points)

- No (0 points)

4) How often do you post content to your Facebook fanpage?

  - 3-5 times per week (10 points)

  - Once per week or less (5 points)

  - Rarely, if ever (0 points)

5) Does your practice have a strategy for effectively using

   Twitter?

  - Yes (10 points)

  - No (0 points)

6) Does your practice's website clearly link to your Facebook and

   Twitter accounts?

  - Yes (10 points)

  - No (0 points)

7) How often do you send e-newsletters to your client base?

- 1-2 times per month (10 points)

- Less than once per month, but more than once per year (5 points)

- Rarely, if ever (0 points)

8) Have you used paid search marketing channels (e.g. Google Ads) to promote your practice?

- Yes (10 points)

- No (0 points)

9) Do you monitor review sites for what your customers are saying about your business?

- Yes (10 points)

- No (0 points)

10) Have you claimed your local listings on Google and Yahoo?

- Yes (10 points)

- No (0 points)

Results:

0-40 Points –You have your work cut out for you. Let's get moving.

40-70 Points - You aren't in bad shape, but there's plenty of room to

improve.

70+ Points – Good work, but you've got to keep moving!

Your Practice's Website

Your practice's website will function as the central component of your online marketing plan. It's your home base. It's where you send new, current, and potential clients when they want more information about your practice. These clients are savvy consumers who are online for much of their time during the day, so they know a good website when they see one.

You might be tempted to think that people will overlook a website that doesn't look good because they'll naturally assume the best about you or your animal hospital. There are two reasons you shouldn't bank on that:

1) Everyone has a patience threshold with websites, and the more they need to think to navigate one, the more likely they are to go elsewhere. Unfortunately for you, your customers use websites everyday that have been designed, tested, and re-designed by user interface (UI), user experience (UX), and web

usability experts so they're extremely easy and enjoyable to navigate. You don't want to give people mental whiplash when they open your site in a browser.

2) People often gauge whether or not they should do business with a company based what their website looks like. And that's not necessarily unfair of them to do. From the perspective of one of your clients, a website that's carefully designed and easy-to-use reflects a company interested in using the latest technologies to make sure their customers are happy. On the other hand, a hospital that doesn't have a working and well-designed website may mean that its owner is either negligent, behind-the-times, or uninterested in making sure clients have a positive experience with the hospital's brand.

A simple comparison

In my experience, it's better to think of your animal hospital's website like a second storefront. Besides the fact that it receives lots of "traffic," it may be the first (and only) place people encounter your

business. If you're still a little peeved that your customers would judge

your animal hospital on the quality of your website, a simple

comparison shows that what they're doing is quite understandable.

Below are two restaurants. You've never seen or eaten at either before.

But if you were to drive by them both in succession, which are you

mostly likely to dine at?

Of course, you'd choose the one on the right. Without ever tasting the food, you know that a restaurant with a poorly maintained exterior is more likely to be operating poorly on the interior. The same goes for your animal hospital and its website—no matter how kind or well-trained your staff is, people don't have a reason to trust you if you don't present yourself respectably online.

Another reason your website needs to be in tip-top shape: it's the destination you drive all of your traffic with online marketing. As you'll see over the next several pages, marketing channels like Google Ads or Facebook are like introductory salesmen who pass potential clients off to your website to close the deal. So If you're working hard to engage customers on Facebook and Twitter, or trying to drive traffic with Google, Yahoo, or Bing, but your website is buggy or difficult to navigate, I hate to say it—but it's all for naught. If your website isn't optimized to help visitors find the information they want to find, it's time to stop spending money on consultants who promise to help you drive traffic to your site.

What makes a good website?

A good website is one that gives clients exactly what they're looking for within 5 seconds of "eye-time" on the page. If you fail to deliver that in 5 seconds, you can bet that the consumer will move on out of frustration and find another practice to do business with. They're just too used to being able to find what they want on the web immediately to be patient with your site that can't do that the same.

So, what exactly are consumers looking for on a veterinary hospital's website?

- *Who you are* - Have staff and doctor bios easy to find. For many of your clients, pets are a part of the family, and they want to know everything they can about who they are bringing these little "family members" to for medical care.

- *What you do* - By listing your services, clients will know immediately whether or not your clinic can meet their needs.

Highlight services that you specialize in to reel in clients with more specialized cases!

- *Pictures of your practice* – Remember the storefront comparison? Show off your practice with a picture gallery. You want clients to know your practice is credible long before they walk in the front door.

- *Your contact information* – In the header or banner, your site should display easy-to-read contact information, including your practice's phone number and a physical street address.

- *A way to get in touch* – Make it easy for a new client to contact you. Have a short form available for new clients to fill out without making them feel like they're giving you too much information.

All in all, keep it simple and clean. Don't overwhelm visitors with too much text or too many pictures—put just enough to satisfy their questions and get them in the front door. At the end of the book, I've included a checklist for you to review your website and make sure it's running on all cylinders.

Now, the elephant in the room: You're a veterinarian. You don't have a clue about web design, and to learn enough to do it yourself could take months. So, as I mentioned previously, there are some areas of online marketing that you should be spending money on, and having a great website should be your first priority in that respect. The reason I've included all of this information is to help you ask the right questions of whoever you hire, to make sure you know that they know what they're doing, and will come up with a design solution that's good for your business.

Your website on mobile devices

As the cost of smartphones and tablets drop year after year, consumers are increasingly using mobile devices to access the Internet. Having a mobile-ready website is another critical opportunity to make the most of your online marketing efforts.

There are two basic versions of mobile websites. The first is just your current website, but optimized for mobile browsers. Clients will have to navigate through the page just as they do on a desktop, but the content will be formatted to fit the screen they're using. The second kind is a simplified template that offers clients only features they'd be likely to access from a mobile device such as:

- Click to Call

- Hours of Operation

- Doctor and Staff Bios

- Click for Directions

- Click for Email Contact

Each option is relatively affordable and easy to develop, but do your practice the favor of making it easy for mobile visitors to find what they're looking for on your website. If you've already built your website, it might be worth talking with your designer about what it would take to create a mobile optimized version. If it was built on WordPress, it's really easy to make a quick version, but if you really want to customize what people see, you'll probably need to spend a

little extra.

Website Best Practices

1. Make it easy for visitors to find information they're likely to

   want.

2. Include staff bios and pictures of the practice.

3. Place your contact information somewhere prominent.

4. Have an appropriate amount of pictures and video content.

5. Make sure the site is optimized for mobile devices.

Search Engine Optimization

I'm sure you've heard about search engine optimization (SEO), or had a consultant at a conference offer to help you improve it. But what is it? And why is it so important? SEO is the practice of optimizing the content on your website to make it easy for sites like Google, Bing, and Yahoo to find. These search engines "crawl" the Internet every minute of every day, assessing the authority of websites all around the world and presenting them in order of relevance to what people search for. When a consumer types in a search term into any of these sites, there is specific algorithm used to determine how and when your website will show up on their screen.

If you want your website to show up when local pet owners search for vet services, there is no need to hire a consultant or SEO professional— you can do it yourself in just a few hours a week. I say this assuming that when your website was built, that it was at least minimally optimized with meta-tags. Make sure you ask whoever puts your site together to take care of this for you.

Here are three simple tips for helping your website rank for searches your clients conduct:

1. Keep an active blog and post unique content to it on a regular basis. Your clients love to hear from your doctors and staff, and there's no better way to do that than with frequent and informative blog posts. Develop a plan for featured staff members to write short articles for the website once or twice a month. Keeping the content fresh and relevant to your clientele will show search engines that your site has valuable information for searchers, thus improving your rankings in search results.

2. Have active Facebook and Twitter accounts that link to your website. Make it easy for clients who follow your practice on these social platforms to click to your website whenever they see a post from you.

3. Link to other pertinent websites from your blog. Partner with other industry professionals who have an online presence by inviting them to write a guest blog post on your website. They will want to link to their article from their site and thus invite others in their network to do the same. In time, links to your practice will be spread across the web, communicating to Google that your site is reputable and deserving of better rankings.

Search Engine Marketing

Search engine marketing (SEM) is an advertising technique where you post ads for your practice on search engines and other websites, paying only when a consumer clicks on these ads. Pay-per-click (PPC) campaigns can be expensive, but if carried out correctly, they can bring very targeted traffic to your website and, in-turn, more business to your hospital.

Here's a basic rundown of how it works: using Google Adwords, you can design a simple text-based ad (a title, description, and website URL) that will show up when people search keywords that describe your business. For example, on Adwords, you can design a text ad that says "An Affordable Animal Hospital in Phoenix" with information about your practice that will show up every time people in Phoenix search "Animal Hospital" on Google. When searchers click on your ad, Google will charge you a pre-set fee, starting at anywhere from a few dollars to much more. Be forewarned that if you're trying to advertise on competitive keywords where other companies are already

advertising, the PPC is going to be higher.

When you're ready, head to http://www.google.com/adwords/ to get

started. There are plenty of tutorials and walk-throughs to help you get

your bearings.

Now, as an aside, in speaking with a number of practice owners across

the country, I've found that they tend to have varied success with SEM.

Some hospitals have seen tremendous results and others seem to see it

as a complete waste of time and money. I took some time and

researched the reasons for such vastly different experiences in a single

industry. As I suspected, the answer was simple: those who had

unsuccessful programs had poor websites.

Again, if you are driving traffic to a website that does not give

consumers what they want, your return on investment (ROI) is not

going to be pretty! Successful programs were driving SEM traffic to

specific landing pages customized to contain exactly what searchers

were looking for. Although this section is primarily about SEM strategies, it underscores the first point I made in this book: having a

high-quality website is central to your online marketing plan.

Social Media Marketing

Social media is here to stay. Why? Because people will always want to connect, share, and keep up with what their friends and associates are doing, and social media sites are focusing on helping them to do it.

Having said that, I think it's important to make something very clear before we get into strategies for specific social networks. That is, if you want to successfully use social media sites for your business, you need to be there for the same reasons everyone else is.

Have you ever been at a party when someone starts shamelessly plugging their own business, giving out business cards, or asking you about who you're using for which services, and so on? It's unbearably awkward. That's because when people come together to be social, they don't want to be sold to.

The reason most clinics fail to gain traction on social media is that they treat social media platforms like another storefront (that's what your website is for!). It's important to remember that your clients are bombarded on a day-to-day basis with sales pitches, banner ads, and billboards, and that they use social media to connect with real people, not to be sold to. The last thing that they want is to follow an animal hospital only to discover that it's just another contributor to the endless stream of advertisements they see every day.

Facebook

If you don't have a Facebook page for your practice by now, get with the program! Setting up a page is simple and it's a great way to connect with your clients and drive traffic to your website.

The key to a successful Facebook presence is engagement. It's all about getting your clients to think about what you have posted and take action. Time and again, I'll be looking through a hospital's Facebook feed and only see sales pitches and boring information. In fact, recently I saw a Facebook post on a Hospital site that said, "Come in and get 20% off of your Pet's dental cleaning during the month of February!" The post had no pictures or links to go with that line—just the practice's telephone number. I can guarantee you that this post generated 0 dental cleaning visits.

If I was a client and I saw this, I would unsubscribe immediately. It offers me nothing but a sales pitch! How would I do it, you ask?

First, I would write a blog post detailing the benefits of regular dental cleanings for pets. At the end of the post, I'd include an exclusive online discount and offer contact information for the client to reach out to.

Next, I'd post a link to the article on Facebook with a cute or fun picture of a pet. When your clients see the article in their newsfeeds they'll see a short summary of the article alongside the picture. If the consumer is interested, they will click through to your site and sign up!

By posting unique content in the form of blog posts, you are offering more than a sales pitch to your followers. You are providing valuable information that engages them much more than a pitch of a product or service.

Another great way to engage your followers is to post polls or trivia questions with a prize offering to those who participate. I recently spoke with a practice manager who posted the following question, "There was a dog on the Navy SEAL team that raided Osama Bin Laden's home last year. What was this dog's name and breed?" Included was a picture of the dog, with a statement that anyone with the right answer would be entered into a drawing for a $25.00 hospital gift card. This hospital only had 250 followers to begin the day, but by the end of the day they had jumped to 525 followers as their fans reposted the question to their personal profiles. Engage your followers with fun questions and you will see results.

I am asked often about the optimal frequency and times of day to post content to Facebook. This is a hotly debated topic within the social marketing community, but a general rule of thumb is that you shouldn't do it more than once a day, and that you should to vary the times of day you post.

If you have trouble finding time every day or remembering to post that often, there are several software solutions out there (HootSuite, for example), which allow you to set up and schedule future posts. It is a reliable tool that helps you stay connected with your fans without as much daily time and attention.

Facebook Checklist

1. Share quality content in status updates.

2. Don't give sales pitches!

3. Ask questions, post polls, and find creative ways to engage with fans.

4. Be pleasant and responsive when people reach out to you on your Facebook page.

5. Provide a link to your blog and website in your fanpage's description section.

6. Don't post too often! Once a day is plenty.

Twitter

Twitter is another helpful tool you can use to engage your clients and ramp up traffic to your site. But the way engagement works on Twitter is quite a bit different from how it works on Facebook and other social networks. What follows is a quick outline of Twitter dynamics and etiquette, along with a few ideas to help you get started.

On Twitter, people follow other people (and businesses) they think have valuable things to say. So, whenever someone that you're following "tweets" out a message (including links, pictures, or videos), what they tweeted will show up on your homepage. Since you're able to follow as many people as you would like, your homepage looks something like a news ticker tape, automatically updating itself whenever someone you follow has tweeted something. From your homepage feed, you have the ability to re-tweet what someone else has tweeted (so your followers will see it), respond directly in a new tweet, or send them a private "direct message." Every communication on Twitter (including direct messages) is limited to 140 characters, so you have to think carefully about what you want to say.

Twitter is built much more around conversations than Facebook is. Whereas fans and brands don't typically have much to say to each other directly on Facebook, Twitter exists for that sort of interaction. Although the rest of this chapter will revolve around how you can use Twitter to interact with your clients, it's worth noting that by following companies and thought leaders in pet care, you'll be able to stay up on the conversations that are happening around the world about your industry.

Twitter has made it very easy to set up what they call a Twitter "handle" which will be your company name after the (@) symbol. For instance, my Twitter handle is @DrewLaine21. Once your account is setup, you will need to make a decision on strategy about how you could interact with your clients, and then set goals for what you'll accomplish with your Twitter account.

Companies in different industries have different reasons for using Twitter. For instance, in the airline industry, marketing and customer service departments have utilized Twitter as a means of receiving feedback and client communication. If a customer is upset that a flight is delayed and expresses their frustration on Twitter, the airline has the opportunity to interact and save the relationship with that customer.

In the veterinary field, there is a hospital on the west coast that has proactively asked their clients for their twitter handles. Then, the hospital uses the platform to communicate with their clients for appointment and compliance reminders, and even happy birthday shout-outs. It has been a great success and their client base has had nothing but positive feedback for the hospital.

Like Facebook, I would advise you to stay away from using your Twitter profile to sell your services! Use it as a tool to communicate, educate and engage your client base.

Twitter Checklist

1. Complete your profile (handle, name, description and images)

2. Include a link to your blog on your profile

3. Interact with other Twitter users—don't just broadcast your practice

4. Follow and learn from industry leaders

5. Keep tweets short and sweet

6. Don't tweet too often! Once or twice a day is plenty.

YouTube

YouTube can be also be great asset to your clinic's online marketing efforts, but it takes a little more expertise, capital, and commitment than Facebook and Twitter do. If you have the resources, setting up a YouTube channel for your hospital and posting videos of procedures, staff bios and even a hospital tour will communicate to your clients that you have a true commitment to being helpful and transparent. For instance, many pet owners are terrified at the thought of putting their pets under anesthesia. But if you posted a video to your YouTube channel explaining the procedure as well as precautions taken by the staff, it would go a long way toward putting them at ease about the idea of anesthetizing their pets.

There's also vast potential for you to educate current and potential clients with YouTube. Since people are increasingly tuning in to YouTube to learn, you'll be able to build authority for your practice and drive traffic by providing tutorials that clearly and succinctly answer people's questions about pet care. Now, before your mind jumps to worrying that you'd be giving out this information for free, it's important to remember, again, that social media is not a platform for sales. It's about relationships. Offering helpful information via tutorials and how-to video content will show your potential clients that you're someone they can trust, and that you've done them a favor. You can guarantee that when they come up against a pet problem they can't solve, they're going to come to you first because they know you and are thankful for how you've helped them already.

LinkedIn

LinkedIn is a social networking site for professionals. It allows you to display your resume online and connect to other professionals through groups and shared associations. What are the varied uses of LinkedIn? Discuss them briefly.

Although, your business is primarily about connecting with consumers and new client finding works best for B2B on LinkedIn, I would challenge you as a practice owner or manager to ask your staff at your next meeting how many of them have LinkedIn profiles. The ideal response would be 100%, but I would estimate that less than half will actually have a profile set up. Why would this matter? As your staff sets up profiles for themselves, your network will grow exponentially. Whenever a staff member approves a connection or a connection approves a staff member's request, your hospital name will show up on their feed. It's a very simple way to get your practice's name in front of more consumers.

Social marketing is a tremendous tool and by following the basic guidelines discussed in this chapter, you will see positive results within your client base.

Conclusion

As I bring this book to a close, I hope that by now you're starting to see what a little elbow grease directed toward online marketing could do to grow your practice. I also hope I've instilled in you enough confidence for you to feel comfortable getting started on your own. You can do it! As for some parting wisdom, keep in mind is that when something feels just a little too tricky for you to do on your own, it's going to be just as tricky for your competitors. Every obstacle you push beyond means you'll have moved that much further beyond another practice owner or manager who wasn't willing to do what you were.

Finally, I think you'll find, as I have, that marketing your own practice is a very satisfying experience. You know the ins and outs of your practice better than anyone else in the world, and you take pride in every procedure you conduct. Who better to be telling the world about it? With consistent effort, I promise that someday you'll look back and be amazed at how far you've come. Good luck!

Great Hospital Website Examples

http://animalhospitaloflynnfield.com/
The Animal Hospital of Lynnfield
Lynnfield, MA

http://irvinevetservices.com/
Irvine Veterinary Services
Irvine, CA

http://www.cottonwoodanimalhospital.com/
Cottonwood Animal Hospital
Salt Lake City, Utah

http://nflah.com/
North Florida Animal Hospital
Tallahassee, Florida

www.ingramcontent.com/pod-product-compliance
Lightning Source LLC
Chambersburg PA
CBHW071126210326
41519CB00020B/6436